DO I GET TO MAKE YOU MINE?

Dr. PRATIK PRAVIN BHAT
(THE DARK POET)

BookLeaf Publishing

India | USA | UK

Presentation by *BookLeaf Publishing*

Web: www.bookleafpub.com

E-mail: info@bookleafpub.com

ISBN: 9789363313514

First edition 2024

For Saumya

Prologue

Upon that fateful day it dawned,
As heavens darkened in the sky,
That I had erred in every way,
Yet, repetition reigned, refusing to comply.

A hoodie draped, an axe in hand,
A blow unto my former flame,
Thus, did I, amidst the shadows stand,
Quenching ghosts, my past to tame.

Yet with each stroke of sharpened steel,
My flesh, in wonder, tore apart,
Ascending higher, a soul to heal,
In a crimson, chaotic art.

Stains of scarlet upon the bed,
Pillowcases awash in red,
Gazing out where heavens spread,
Blue fading to black, as if it bled.

In flames, my spirit seemed to ignite,
Would this day see my survival,
Or shall I succumb to an endless night,
A victim bound, a slave to revival?

Then came the cold, a jolt of water's touch,
Drenched and shivering, from dreams untold,
Reality's grip, though I would clutch,
Yet still, my thoughts in darkness fold.

"Mother!", her voice, a beacon near,
She who I cherished, for whom I lived,
"You trembled as if a hummingbird", her words
clear,
Awakening me from dreams contrived.

Disturbed by memories, haunting and grim,
Rahul, a spectre, haunting my core,
A vow I made, to banish him,
Yet like lingering scent, he lingers more.

Upon the floor, my sickness spilled,
My mother, with mop, began to tend,
Yet what of my soul, still unfulfilled,
In this torment, will it find an end?

Part I

Seeking Serenity

In Church Street, I strolled one morning,
A Starbucks close by, a roadside stall for filter
coffee too,
Naturally, I chose the filter,
But as I walked, I stumbled,
A stone struck my foot,
Nearly causing me to bang my head,
Recalling my path, I hesitated,
Had I endured enough of being a doctor?
I dreaded the thought of returning to the
hospital.
Would a vacation offer solace,
Or usher in permanent disaster?

A roadside Samaritan aided me to my feet,
I expressed gratitude; his gaze seemed profound.
In return, I offered him filter coffee.
"I don't drink coffee," he replied, then departed.
"Very well," I said, masking my disappointment,
And proceeded to sip the filter coffee, seeking
solace.

With each sip, memories flooded back,
Recollections of past relationships,

Wherein I perennially found myself as the
victim.
My phone interrupted my reverie,
Displaying "ICU" on the screen.
I answered the call and hurried away,
The cup still half full, duty beckoned.

While en route, I pondered places to visit near
Karnataka.
"Goa" topped the list,
And I knew where my next destination lay.
December's end was set for my getaway,
Hoping a vacation might mend my fractured
spirit,
Though uncertain if it would truly heal me.

All I craved was sunlight and sea breeze,
As the cab pulled up, I donned my apron,
Rushing to attend to the ailing patient, whose
patience wore thin.
I allowed my thoughts to wander,
Dreaming of distant shores.

Shattered Promises

In my vision, I found myself
Linked with a man, a famed surgeon,
For just one fleeting night,
We shared our moments,
Fought through our interspersed destinies,
But beneath the guise of universal allure,
We glimmered like unexploded dynamite,
Awaiting ignition.

Yet, he departed abruptly,
Transferred to distant shores,
Leaving without a word,
Leaving me feeling used,
A familiar ache, a recurring theme.
I believed we were more,
For I was devoted, faithful to a fault,
But like those before him,
He relegated me to insignificance,
And I spiralled into despair.

My psychiatrist labelled me unstable,
The pills I sought offered little solace,
So I turned to nicotine-laden cigarettes,
Preferring their bitter comfort.
Alcohol offered no respite,

Clashing with my medication,
Further blurring the lines of reality.

Betrayed repeatedly, I lost myself,
An intensivist, stabilizing others,
Yet adrift in my own sea of turmoil.
He, the surgeon, whispered promises,
Of marriage, of children we'd bear,
But those words vanished with him,
Lost in the streets of London,
Chasing a dream that would never be mine.

Left shattered, scattered like fragments,
No one could mend me, not even I,
In pieces beyond repair,
As the final boarding call resounded online,
My numbness deepened,
Amid the chaos within.

Was there ever time for rest?
To sleep, not just with closed eyes,
But to find solace for my weary soul,
Since my father's untimely demise,
One year ago in a tragic collision,
A bottle of whiskey, a failed brake,
A truck, a life crushed beyond recognition.

Oh, how I miss you, Dad!

This tale of anguish and loss,
In hopes it resonates,
With those who seek solace,
In the depths of shared sorrow.

Destination Untouched

Turbulent skies,
Nausea rising once more,
A bag clutched tightly,
Turbulence overwhelming,
Prayers whispered fervently,
Finally, we touched down,
Safety at last.

The taxi driver grinned knowingly,
Lifting my burden into the boot,
Weightier than myself,
I settled in, propping my keister on the seat,
As we embarked for Anjuna,
My sanctuary, an Airbnb oasis.

Welcomed by a gracious hostess,
Croissant and macchiato awaited,
Requesting more milk until it turned to latte,
I savoured each sip,
Surrounded by verdant paddy fields,
Coconut trees reaching for the sky,
Away from the urban sprawl,
Peace embraced my soul.

To the beach, I urged the driver,
Another grin, another journey,
But as my phone chimed,
"ICU Ward Sister" flashed across the screen,
Even on vacation, duty calls.

Enlisting a friend to manage the call,
I silenced my device,
Tossing it into the seat pocket,
Determined to immerse myself
In the unparalleled beauty before me.

In this paradise, my heart found tranquillity,
Perhaps here, I'd remain forever.
Popping another pill,
As prescribed by my psychiatrist,
I hesitated, then discarded the jar of candies,
Realizing therapy lay not in artificial means,
But in the embrace of Goa itself,
Where reality transcended all.

The Beachside Rescuer

Dumped unceremoniously at the beach,
The cab driver's grin faded as I haggled,
Navigating through unforeseen fare,
Anjuna, oh so green,
The sand, vibrant beneath my feet,
This place held a special grip on my soul,
Renowned as a haven for hippies,
Shacks dotted the shoreline,
Trance and techno melodies echoed in the
background.

Choosing one at random,
I let loose, allowing my hair to fall free,
Sipping on a beer, I observed the waves,
Then slipped into my swimwear, a pink
monokini,
Baring myself to the sun and sea,
As I waded into the water,
The tide seized me, pulling me under,
Panic rose within me, "Help!" I cried,
Water flooding my senses,
Drowning in its merciless grasp.

Just as despair threatened to consume me,
A warm presence enveloped my waist,

Guiding me through the tumultuous waves,
A hand, firm and reassuring,
Resisted the pull of the ocean,
Until, at last, I was brought to shore,
Kissed back to life by the sea's reluctant
embrace.

Though the protocols of Cardio Pulmonary
Resuscitation may have evolved,
My body was kissed, jolted and caressed,
Regurgitating water and sand,
As I returned to consciousness, mortified.

Before me stood my saviour,
With curly locks framing a well-defined chest,
Chiselled jawline and formidable abs,
Bronzed by the sun, shoulders broad,
Perhaps the kiss had worked its magic,
For as I gazed into his eyes, I saw his lip part,
Inquiring, "Are you okay, Miss?"

And in that moment, overwhelmed,
Fatigue enveloped me,
Dragging me into unconsciousness once more.

IV-Lines and him

I awoke that day
In the desert breeze of the ward,
Adjacent to the beach,
My hand adorned with an IV-line,
Surveying my unfamiliar surroundings,
My heart, now a submarine,
Longing for the peace of nature's ravine.

"You only need hydration," remarked the
curly-haired figure,
"Good to see you awake. My name is Rahul, and
I harbour no negative demeanour."

His curls stirred memories of another,
The man who had taken my breath away,
With a gentle caress upon my forehead,
Taming my dishevelled locks to perfection,
His warmth embracing me like a comforting
hug,
A sweet gesture in his mere presence.

But our moment was fleeting,
Interrupted by the nurse's intervention,
Requesting Rahul's departure to afford me rest,
Despite my assertion of being a doctor.

"It doesn't matter," she countered firmly,
"Hospital rules are rules. Rahul, back to his
lifeguard duties."

"Lifeguard?" I asked, puzzled by the revelation.

As Rahul bid farewell, the nurse's grin spoke
volumes,
Her success in temporarily parting us,
Leaving me to ponder whether to seek out my
saviour,
Uncertain if I truly knew him beyond that single
moment.

In my turmoil, I pulled at the IV,
Feeling the sting of the needle and the trickle of
blood,
Yet sinking deeper into numbness and slumber,
As the hospital hummed around me,
Enfolding me in its comforting embrace.

Stepping Towards Him

I returned to my room,
Only to be ushered back with an ambulance.
Goan healthcare proved impeccable,
Nurturing me back to health,
I felt reborn, like a baby anew,
Eager to explore the world once more.

Sand and sea beckoned, but what of the man to
thank?
The curly-haired, chiselled perfection,
A lifeguard who had risked his own life for
mine,
I felt compelled to show my gratitude.

At a nearby gift shop, a piece of art caught my
eye,
Resembling a keloid, with a black centre and
lavender outline,
Amorphous and evocative,
It stirred within me a tumult of emotions.
As I studied it further, I discerned more than just
sadness,
The name "S" signed below the artwork,
Intrigued, I wondered about the artist's identity.

The artwork, with its dark humour and despair,
Challenged my perceptions,
Yet in the chaos, I spotted teddies, books, and
robots,
A semblance of normalcy in the turmoil.
Would Rahul appreciate the keloid, I pondered,
Only time would reveal.

Requesting the shopkeeper to package the piece,
I felt his scrutinizing gaze,
Unfazed, I wore a Maroon Deep-V knitted Mini
dress,
A defiant expression against the melancholy of
hospital gowns.
I revelled in self-expression,
My body, a canvas for the world to behold.

With the parcel in hand,
"I hope my saviour appreciates it," I murmured,
Treading my path cautiously,
Avoiding the water's edge, resolved not to risk
further peril.

Arriving at a nearby coffee shop,
I indulged in a warm Americano,
Accompanied by the familiar scent of ash,
A reminder of our transient existence,
As fleeting as smoke dispersing into the air.

I Treaded The Beaten Path

In the haze of smoke, I found myself,
Maroon-clad, before the mirror's stealth.
Adjusting my attire, snug and tight,
Seeking seduction in the curves of night.

A gift wrapped in glitter, golden gleam,
In hand, I venture to dreams unseen.
Outside, the beach, my haven, my quest,
Yet he, the one, eludes my behest.

A stranger's guidance leads my gaze
To cliffs of rocky, cinnamon haze.
There, a figure, high and free,
Leaps, catches vines, and descends to me.

"Ananya," he speaks, whispering my name,
How he knows, I dare not claim.
Mellow his aura, calming my fear,
As I stand entranced, his presence near.

Nicotine stains upon his lips,
A cape adorns, like a superhero's scripts.
Half-pants worn, scent of beer in air,
Yet his gaze holds me, unaware.

Into the abyss of shadowed trance,
My mind wanders, lost in chance.
A necklace of rope, a tooth displayed,
Silver ring, boots in moss arrayed.

He saved my life, this man of might,
"I've brought you a gift," she offers light.
Surprised, he frowns at my glittering fare,
"Is it not to your liking?" she dares.

With a glance, he sees beyond,
Unmoved by trinkets, artful bond.
"It's 'S' for Saddie, my nickname" he reveals,
A maker of art, the soul that heals.

Another layer to this enigmatic man,
Creativity's wisdom, an eternal plan.
In his essence, something more,
A depth of spirit, to explore.

Exploring the Locus of Passion

He gazes at the keloid, holds it close to his heart,
His own artwork gifted, a profound piece of art.
He takes my hand, specifically the right,
His grasp firm, his touch igniting a cosmic light.

"May I take you," he asks, "on a ride upon my
bike?"
A kilometre away, he reveals where he resides.
A grand house with a garden, a sight to behold,
And within, a shed where his mysteries unfold.

Canvases adorned with melancholy's aura,
Paints splashed, deer headless, invoking a
fervour.
Wooden dolls, fingers amiss, a sight to intrigue,
A giant snowman, its belly gaunt, a mystique.

A vampire atop a werewolf, in a world of his
own,
Keloid-like mould, a place with creatures
overthrown.

Honey bees and insects embalmed, beetle cut in
half,
Stuffed animals and heads, a scene to baffle and
laugh.

There's something askew, yet compellingly
divine,
In the mind of an artist, where boundaries aren't
defined.
Creative indulgence, not for the faint-hearted
soul,
As I gaze upon his work, emotions take their
toll.

A boy gripping his mother's hand at a fair,
Her eyes black, devoid of white, an eerie stare.
The child faceless, nose inverted, a disturbing
sight,
"This is my artwork," he reveals, seeking
insight.

"It has caused me shock," I utter, surprised by
his depth,
As we dive into realms where sanity has left.
"Do you fancy drawing?" he asks, drawing near,
Placing a brush in my hand, a canvas clear.

Our hands move in sync, a dance of creation,
My inner space gripped by a newfound
sensation.
Drawing a planet from the outer expanse,
He praises my skill, his eyes filled with trance.

"I won't stay long," I confess, feeling salvation,
Exchanging numbers, a fleeting sensation.
"It's time for my tour to South Goa," I sigh,
Yet he kneels, drawing me closer with a high.

"Let's have coffee," he suggests, his eyes
gleaming bright,
At 'Fire and Ice', we sip, engulfed in the night.
"How long will you stay?" he inquires with
hope,
"Just five days," I reply, emotions a tightrope.

He drops me back, duty calls him, we part with a
vow,
"We'll meet again," he assures, hope in the now.
The taxi driver grins, as I watch Rahul depart,
In that moment, I decide to follow my heart.

I cancel the trip, much to the driver's dismay,
All I desire is to be where he stays.
I pocket a stone from his workshop, shaped like
a bear,
A reminder of him, with wild hair and care.

In the depths of uncertainty, love finds its way,
In the artist's embrace, where emotions sway.
With each stroke of the brush, our souls connect,
In a world of art and passion, a love divine
intersects.

An Ode to Serendipity

I dared to ask him once more,
Why everything was signed "S"?
He spoke of a nickname,
"Saddie Rahul," a remnant of childhood,
Where sadness cloaked his serious stare,
And smiles were a rare treasure.

Longing gripped my heart,
Prompting a call, an innate urge,
"How's the south of Goa? So wondrous, so
mystique."
"I didn't venture there today, for reasons
unknown to me."
"A crying shame," he remarked,
And laughter danced between us.

I wished for him to take the lead,
"Shall dinner be on me?" he offered,
And thus, plans were made,
For a seaside meal in a humble shack.

As we bid farewell on the phone,
The promise of 8 PM hung in the air,
A rendezvous on his bike,
Lost in our musings, we'd journey.

Curiosity stirred within me,
His artwork had cast a spell,
But who was the man behind the facade?
Beneath the delicate eggshell exterior.

I turned to Google, seeking perfection,
A beauty parlour reserved for señoritas,
I needed to present my best self,
Though the motivation eluded me.

The emerald one-piece dress,
With its intricate floral design,
A symbol of elegance and temptation,
Woven to captivate his fascination.

As the days dwindled down,
And my return to Bangalore loomed near,
I knew I would miss Rahul deeply,
Yet tonight would be a memory to cherish,
A memory, indeed, to keep.

Journeys Through Memories and Past Lives

The parlour worked wonders,
How wrong I was to doubt my beauty.
"Body Dysmorphia," my psychiatrist explained,
A fancy term for undue mental distress.

At the reception, I awaited him,
Busy reshaping my perception.
In school, I stood,
Stained by my first period's arrival,
A white uniform marred,
As I cried for help,
In between mocking whispers.

Trauma lingered,
Etched in the corridors of memory,
Yet I stood strong,
Though shattered in pieces,
Struggling to find sobriety.

In medical school, a boy emerged,
Pulling me from the crowd,
His support a pillar of strength,
As he waged battles for my honour,

And led me to a fort,
Where we surrendered to passion,
In the embrace of a nature's beauty,
Beneath starlit skies.

Yet, the next day brought betrayal,
A video circulated,
His Point of View,
Capturing my surrender,
In virtual reality,
A sin upon my soul,
I confronted him,
His smirk a mockery of remorse,
As he revelled in his conquest.

Devastation enveloped me,
Used and discarded,
Silenced by shame,
I drowned in smoke and liquor,
Avoiding the prying eyes of judgment.

But courage surged within,
Confronting the man,
Pushing him against the wall,
Demanding justice for my violated dignity.

His skinny frame trembled,
As I stripped him of his facade,
Exposing the truth,

Recording his humiliation,
And sending it to the masses.

Silence fell over the crowd,
Dumbfounded by the reversal of power,
As he begged for forgiveness,
While I walked away,
A triumphant laughter echoing in my wake.

In harmony, I reclaimed my strength,
My fate saved by me.

Navigating Into The Unknown

As a honk shattered the stillness,
I wrestled free from the clutches of the past,
My pills forgotten, thoughts swirling endlessly.

Stepping outside, I beheld him,
Clad in a sleek blue slim-fit tuxedo,
A transformation from lifeguard to model,
Leaving me pondering his intentions.

The tux accentuated his physique,
His chest broad, his waist narrow,
His gaze piercing, his demeanour energetic.

He whisked me away to a sea-side shack,
Where beer flowed freely,
And shrimps adorned our plates,
An everyday luxury befitting a lifeguard turned
artist.

"My art sells too," he proclaimed redundantly,
Revealing his online portfolio,
Rooted in his lifeguard lineage,
Granting him moments of contemplation.

With breath warm upon my cheek,
He drew near, but withheld the kiss,
Instead, a gentle touch, a stray hair adjusted,
Leaving me adrift in uncertainty.

A phone call interrupted our reverie,
His "wife," I happened to see,
Etched upon the screen,
Questions swirled within, unspoken,
As I chose to play the role of ignorance.

Returning to the table, he proposed a party,
His enthusiasm contagious,
Despite the incongruity of his attire.

"I've got the moves, baby," he assured,
His words mingling with the discord of my
thoughts,
A melody of doubt and desire,
In the layers of intrigue.

Journey Into The Rave

I sat behind him, adoringly,
Though my hands remained aloft,
A silent acknowledgment of boundaries.
The revelation of his wife lingered,
A looped DVD in my mind,
Yet we settled into the role of buddies.

"Ouch!" A bump disrupted our reverie,
Shaking my transient existence,
But we shared a smile,
As if disaster were our constant companion.

Arriving at the jetty,
A club on the edge,
I dismounted from his bike,
His gaze lingering on me.

"You never cease to amaze," he remarked,
His words a balm to my thoughts,
Yet questions of his wife remained unspoken,
Lost in the moon's ethereal glow,
I felt like a werewolf, longing to change.

"Shall we enter?" he proposed,
A fine dining experience replaced by club
ambiance,
His smile coaxing me forward,
Filling the blank spaces between us.

Inside, the music enveloped us,
Seducing our souls with its rhythm,
Beer in hand, we surrendered to the dance,
Each movement synchronized; every beat
captured.

Another beer, another moment lost,
As he enveloped me in his grasp,
His breath warm against my neck,
A tangible connection, electric and raw.

Dancing and intoxication blurred the lines,
We became the stars of the night,
Lost in each other's orbit,
Unnoticed in the revelry.

As dawn approached, the party continued,
Our bodies moving in harmony,
An unspoken understanding guiding us,
Despite the absence of a kiss.

In the quiet of the early morning,
We found relief in shared cigarettes and beers,

His touch igniting a fire within,
As tears flowed freely, revealing my heart's
truth.

I confessed my gratitude,
For his presence during my darkest hours,
For the kiss that brought me back to life,
And the intimacy that followed.

He confessed his own struggle,
With the rules of CPR and the pull of desire,
Yet, despite knowing the guidelines,
He couldn't resist the temptation of my beauty,
A moment suspended in time,
In the quiet tranquillity of the breaking dawn.

And in whispered tones, he revealed,
That he had divorced his wife,
Setting us both free to explore,
The depths of our connection,
In the eternity of the night.

Awakening To The First Kiss

Drawing nearer to him,
The floor trembled beneath our touch,
Resting my head upon his shoulder,
Finding sublime pleasure in his comforting
embrace.

His fingers delicately jigsawed with mine,
As he tenderly brushed my forehead with his
lips,
"Let's go," he whispered,
Guiding me with a gentle hand.

I surrendered to his lead,
As we witnessed the sun's ascent,
Walking along the golden sands,
My heart mirroring the hues of dawn.

His gaze bore into mine,
Pulling me closer,
I rose onto my toes,
Seeking to meet his height,
Yet he bent down in perfect synchrony,
And his lips met mine in a tender kiss.

At first, a gentle peck,
But soon, our breaths deepened,
Time slowed as we savoured each moment,
Our souls connected and drawn into the horizon.

Pressed against his chest,
His embrace engulfing me,
Our kisses grew deeper,
Exploring the depths of desire.

Lost in passion's embrace,
We touched each other with flavour,
Laying upon the beach,
Lost in the rhythm of our shared passion.

Yet, the intrusive sound of a phone shattered our
reverie,
"Wife" flashed across the screen,
And doubt clouded my mind,
If he had divorced, why still keep it as such?

Retreating, I fled,
His apologies trailing behind me,
But I had already summoned a cab,
My resolve to depart outweighing the lingering
love.

For in the embrace of sunrise,
I found calmness in the storm,

But love would only lead to further decay,
As I sought refuge in sleep,
Leaving behind the remnants of our passion,
On the shores of regret.

Whispers Of Doubt

A persistent phone call disrupted my solitude,
Each ring a reminder of unanswered questions,
Switching it off, I sought cheer in isolation,
Reflecting on why I chose to date him,
If this was only a web of lies.

As evening descended, I relented,
Preparing for tomorrow's journey homeward,
The final day in Goa, laden with memories,
Both cherished and painful,
Yearning for Bangalore, my home, silent retreat.

But in the quiet, my phone beeps resounded,
A desperate plea for salvation,
Yet, who would rescue me from myself?

His messages flooded in, begging for
forgiveness,
Claiming he had indeed divorced her,
An attachment unveiled the certificate,
The name Shanaya, a whisper of magic,
Was she the elusive "S" in his life?

Turning to Instagram, I sought answers,
Her account shrouded in privacy,
A request sent, a plea for clarity.

Searching his name yielded similar results,
His profile veiled from scrutiny,
Another request, another hope for truth.

As his artwork flooded my feed,
Strange and surreptitious, much like his studio,
A bell rang, signalling a visitor,
I opened the door to Rahul, his eyes betraying
turmoil,
An apology for my abandonment hung between
us,
And so, I dared to inquire about his wife.

Enthrallment and Revelations

As he entered, a tempest stirred within me,
Uncorking a bottle of wine with practiced ease,
His presence commanding attention,
Pouring crimson ambrosia, an elixir of passion,
Each sip a prelude to our shared desire.

We drank deeply, lost in the dance of
conversation,
His confessions of betrayal a flame to my
longing,
Years of solitude, an eternity without devotion,
His heart yearning for redemption in
companionship,
A desire to marry, unquenched without progeny,
His eyes, a window to his soul, bringing me
closer.

Taking his hand, I offered a gentle kiss,
Our lips met with a bond born of hunger,
His touch a sanctuary, drawing me into the
abyss,
Lost in the depths of his sensations, I
surrendered,

Urging him to explore the depths of my desires,
Each caress a testament to his fervent obsession,
As our bodies mingled in a symphony of ecstasy.

With a primal hunger, he tore away my emerald
dress,
Each thread a sacrifice to our insatiable lust,
His touch igniting sparks of electricity within
me,
As we danced on the precipice of madness.

Thrown onto the bed, we became one,
Exploring every inch of each other's flesh,
Ripping away inhibitions, shedding layers of
restraint,
Our bodies like archaic animals in their
primitive element,
Each moan an orchestration of pleasure, echoing
in the night,
As we surrendered to the rapture of our desire,
Bound by the chains of our shared fascination.

Time ceased to exist as we lost ourselves in each
other,
Every kiss a declaration of undying devotion,
Every touch a promise of perpetual
enlightenment,
As we merged into the inferno of our awakened
desire.

In the aftermath, our hearts beat as one,
Wrapped in the afterglow of our shared fantasy,
Yet, in the bliss, a tinge of doubt lingered,
As he dressed and left, his lifeguard duties
calling him away.

In the silence of the room, revelation struck,
His tattoo, Shanaya, etched like a scar upon his
flesh,
A reminder of a love lost, a ghost haunting his
soul,
As I lay alone, consumed by the thoughts of
what had transpired,
His departure leaving me wanting for more,
Aching for the touch of his fiery existence,
As I waited in the darkness, craving his return,
Flashback of the memory of what we just had,
And the truth revealed in the aftermath of our
enthrallment.

Shanaya And The Follow Request

The request was accepted,
I headed to the washroom,
Taking relief on the seat,
In my own comfort.

I observed as it seeped,
Just two photos adorned the account,
A lady, radiant and handsome,
Resembling dusk till dawn.

Clad in a black saree,
Her eyes averted,
As if gripped by fear,
Perched on a chair,
Anxiety lingering in the air.

The backdrop, a mansion,
With walls akin to the art studio's,
The recent photo depicted,
A sky painted with stars.

The caption read,
"I wish to end my life and be a star,

Not in this mansion,"
In a quote unquote style.

Something foul was afoot,
Should I reach out? I pondered,
Perhaps a simple "Hi" wouldn't hurt,
Yet, no response came.

So, I silenced my phone,
And proceeded to cleanse myself,
In the bath, washing away my deeds,
But was I falling in love,
And at what cost?

I dried myself, approaching the mirror,
Gazing at my bare face,
Unadorned by makeup,
A scar from a past relation inscribed upon it.

My cheeks once bitten by a dog,
By a malevolent man, rejected,
Who seduced me into his bed,
Using me like a tool.

Accusing me of infidelity,
Striking me with violence,
"I'll ruin your face, Bitch," he spat,
Aimed for my lips, hitting my cheek.

I screamed in anguish,
Abused multiple times,
How could I let such horrors befall me?
The lacerations stitched,
But the scar remained unstitched.

Sinking to the floor,
I turned on the shower once more,
Cleansing my body,
But who would cleanse my soul?

Venturing to the wine cellar,
Fetching my whiskey,
Drinking today, drinking tomorrow,
Judged even by my psychiatrist.

Turning to my phone,
Searching for Shanaya,
A received message and an unsent one,
Now blocked from her profile.

Mind-blown, unable to comprehend,
I turned to Rahul's profile,
Shanaya absent from his pictures,
Not a mutual friend from the start.

She had assumed it was an uncomfortable
divorce,
Husband and wife blocking each other,

From their respective accounts,
The whiskey aiding my memories.

                    45

As smoke curled into the air,
I touched myself, recalling our passionate affair,
Rahul! I miss you too much,
To succumb to my own despair.

I Leave As He Leaves Me

Today marks my final day,
A night flight takes me away,
Hoping for change, though fleeting it seems,
Knowing such moments fade like dreams.

Rahul claimed his time was tight,
Yet after our embrace, vanished from sight,
Dialling his number, hoping to find,
But alas, the end seemed near, unkind.

Bags packed, ready to go,
I ventured to a flower store, you know,
Amongst the roses, thorns concealed,
I chose one with thorns that his heart would
yield.

To his door I made my way,
Longing for love's sweet array,
But alas, at five, the house stood shut,
The art studio barren, devoid of his strut.

Inquiries made, yet no one knew,
Where Rahul went, no clue to construe,
With a flight to catch, tears I shed,
Who was this man, by what name was he led?

Time fleeting, no answers found,
Into a taxi, I was bound,
The New Year's Eve, irony profound,
Instagram's message, a puzzle unwound.

"Help me!" it pleaded, nameless, forlorn,
No Shanaya, no voice, just a digital thorn,
Blocked from my grasp, the account crased,
Leaving behind "Instagram User," a ghostly
trace.

Deeming it spam, I turned away,
To the airport, where my journey lay,
Bound for Bangalore, yet my heart in tow,
Saddie Baddie Rahul, I'll miss you so,
And Anjuna's shores, where memories flow,
In Goa's embrace, where dreams used to grow.

Part II

Navigating Through Life

In Bangalore once more,
I donned my shades,
Stepping into the uninhibited horizon,
Where the cab driver awaited,
Online apps, a blessing for sure.

A mundane day it seemed,
Routine like all the rest,
Emergencies at the hospital,
Where my expertise lies best,
Stabilizing airway, breathing, circulation,
My daily quest.

Six months since Goa's embrace,
No word from Rahul, no trace,
No new artwork adorned his space,
Was he alive, or had he found his peace?

Desire to find him gnawed within,
But avenues to pursue grew thin,
A longing to return to Goa's shores,
Perhaps lodge a police complaint, implores.

But what crime had he committed?
In our consensual affair, was he acquitted?

Yet, a new companion I'd found,
An anorexic, bisexual confidant, profound.

He shared tales of his life's ventures,
With pride, his thin chest he presents,
A Casualty Medical Officer by trade,
Unmarried, well-to-do, our lives serenade.

Belonging to the same clan, fate aligned,
Our parents' approval we would find,
In the canteen, we'd sit side by side,
Phones buzzing as emergencies bide.

In life's hustle, we found ourselves,
Surrounded by turmoil, a reassuring hug
Trying to move on from Rahul's absence,
Yet his memory lingered, a haunting presence.

But this new companion, gentle and kind,
A soothing balm to the heart and mind,
In our thirties, we navigate life's demands,
Health concerns and uncertainties, life's
commands.

Children never a necessity, yet now a thought,
Ovulatory cycles wane, as time is sought,
The world keeps spinning, waits for none,
As my biological clock ticks, thoughts overrun.

Medications prescribed, my psychiatrist's decree,
To stabilize the chaos within me,
Skipping doses, a dangerous flirtation,
In a world painted red and blue, a sensation.

Descending onto stability's divine plane,
Rahul's absence a constant refrain,
Yet hope flickers in this newfound love,
A proposal awaited, sent from above.

Lavender roses and black vampires in tow,
Symbols of love, to cherish and sow,
As medication and stability intermingle,
Rahul's memory, a ghost in my mind.

"Let's go to Nandi Hills, embrace nature's grace!"
The anorexic man exclaimed, his face,
"Sure," I replied, uncertain of all else,
In life's tempest, nature's cradle, an aid, in trials.

Nandi Hills And Love

In the year 2024, where love knows no bounds,
Anorexic, bisexual, our hearts unbound.
As a doctor, society's attire I wear,
Yet with you, tradition's chains I dare to tear.

Booking a rickshaw, an old man's whispered
fare,
Nandi Hills, beyond the reach of any app, we
accept with care.
A bumpy ride, edging to the borderline
Destination uncertain, yet our love
positive-inclined.

Stopping for Idli, a random delight,
Sharing laughs and bites, our hearts take flight.
Resuming our journey, the hills in sight,
An accident halts us, a Mercedes and a truck
collide
"Do you like me?" you ask, your question feels
right.

In the traffic confusion, with a cigarette lit,
I confess my feelings, unsure but fit.
"I may not know if I like you," I say,
"But stuck in traffic, with you, I want to stay."

Your sad gaze, like a child's toy taken,
My past with Rahul, a monster awakens.
Excusing myself, I seek finding myself in
smoke,
Lost in thoughts, your love I invoke.

As you come near, I blow smoke in the air,
Police arrive, the road clears, love's affair.
The city's distant lights, our journey's end near,
Together, in love, our hearts finally clear.

Hymn To The Hills: An Ode To Nature's Majesty

In the realm where the earth meets the sky,
Nandi Hills, where nature's beauty lies.
Majestic peaks, kissed by the sun's golden hue,
A sanctuary for souls, both old and new.

Upon these hills, a symphony of sights and
sounds,
Whispers of the wind, and birdsongs abound.
The rustling leaves, a soothing melody,
In nature's embrace, hearts find serenity.

Beneath the azure canopy, a canvas divine,
Where colours dance, and dreams align.
Sunrise paints the sky in hues of fire,
A breathtaking sight, to fulfil desire.

As dawn breaks, unveiling the day's grandeur,
The hills awaken, in nature's tender nurture.
Gentle slopes, adorned with verdant green,
A tranquil haven, like never before seen.

Among the valleys and rolling hills,
Nature's beauty, a cure for all ills.

In every flower's bloom and every tree's sway,
A healing power, to light the way.

Here, in the whispers of the ancient trees,
Spirits soar and souls find peace.
Nandi Hills, where nature reigns supreme,
A reservation of beauty, like in a dream.

So come, wanderer, and let your soul unfurl,
In the arms of nature, let your troubles swirl.
For on Nandi Hills, the earth and sky,
You'll find beauty, where dreams can fly.

Emerging from contemplations deep,
We reach the peak, where dreams do keep.
At the parking, our journey halts,
In nature's embrace, our spirit exalts.

We Did It There

From the parking lot, we ascend,
Hand in hand, through the mountain's clasp we
blend.
Bench after bench, couples melt,
Kissing passionately, their love not quelled.

Entering the temple, an unexpected delight,
The Pandit blesses, assuming our love's height.
A good omen, a divine sign,
As breathtaking views and skies align.

Praying for rain, the sun's fiery glare,
Suddenly explodes into a torrential affair.
Rivulets and floods in the sky's domain,
We seek shelter from the rain.

Under an abandoned rusty roof,
Petrichor fills the air, a sensory aloof.
Out of boundaries, senses soar,
As Mr. Anorexic surprises, opening a door.

A joint in hand, in the rain's descent,
We smoke, high as the heavens bent.
Lost in euphoria, senses ablaze,
As raindrops tingle, in a sensual haze.

In the abandoned house, our passions inflamed,
Amidst the rust and shadows, our desires take
flight.
His touch, like fire, sets my soul aflame,
Within the intense grasp of ardour, we inscribe
our identity.

Cultivated in love, moaning whispers and sighs,
Bodies entangled, beneath the brightening skies.
Ecstatic sounds released, in the daylight's grace,
As climax envelops us, pure grace.

But then, at the cliff's edge, a masked figure
appears,
Pushing Mr. Anorexic, my worst fears.
Over the cliff, into eternity's call,
Lost to the depths, a sudden fall.

In shock, I scream, alone in the rain,
The masked man's hammer, a relentless bane.
Running, tripping, falling fast,
Darkness descends, a sudden contrast.

Uncertain, lost in a dream,
Sensations heightened, as reality teems.
Dreams of Rahul, melancholy reigns,
In the rain's embrace, in nature's pains.

As consciousness fades and darkness takes hold,
The question lingers: will my story unfold?
Was I dead, or would I wake to see the light?
And what of Mr. Anorexic, lost to the night?

The masked man's blow, a cruel twist of fate,
Leaves my future uncertain, sealed by hate.
Will I survive, or be the next to fall?
In this tale of mystery, I await destiny's call.

Where am I?

"Mr. Anorexic? Are you alive?"
Regret floods as fear takes a drive.
The hills, a scenic trap, it seems,
Where dreams unravel and nightmares gleam.

Seized by convulsions, life ebbs and flows,
Yet I'm brought back from where darkness
grows.
Awakening to a surreal sight,
An art studio, bathed in eerie light.

Confusion reigns, where am I now?
In Bangalore, or somewhere far somehow?
Bound to a piling, hands gone numb,
Thirst consumes, lips cracked, feeling glum.

A dog bowl holds salvation's kiss,
I lap at water, in pure bliss.
But tension mounts, the air shifts tense,
As footsteps echo, a dark suspense.

Creaking wood, ajar the door,
In shadows cast, fear I abhor.
A figure looms, black as night,
Horns protruding, a chilling sight.

A statue of a Satanic monster, his face aglow,
Overseeing this twisted tableau.

Could I be but a sacrifice, a pawn,
In this captor's twisted dawn?
The door swings open, revealing fate,
A silhouette, sealing my state.

A click, a reveal, a face I know,
Shanaya's visage, in eerie glow.
"Oh yes," she murmurs, a rhythm divine,
In her eyes, madness seeks rewind.

Shanaya

"I had warned my husband, Do not fuck with
that whore,
You appear wholesome, what did he gain, what
for?
Though he told you we're divorced, see this ring,
We're as close as intercourse, my love, my
everything."

The diamond ring gleamed, even in the dim
light,
But in its brilliance, a scene took flight.
The door swung open, and there he stood,
"Rahul?!" I cried, in shock I could.

"Please, control your emotions," he addressed
his wife,
Confusion and tension marred the strife.
"Why am I caught in this bizarre affair?
What's the meaning of this, why are you here?"

Rahul approached with concern in his gaze,
But his attempt to kiss me, I had to raise.
Inappropriate, unwelcome, his advance,
Back to his wife, they began their dance.

"I was never divorced," Rahul declared with a
sneer,
"We lure in lone tourists, without fear."
With a whip in hand, he struck Shanaya sore,
And she moaned in pleasure, craving more.

In this twisted scene, darkness took flight,
As desires warped, and wrong became right.
Caught in their web, I watched in dismay,
Trapped in their game, with no words to say.

Things Unseen And Twisted

What was I even looking at then,
As the truth unveiled, the darkness within men.
"We must offer our deity a sacrificial lamb,
Babies are too risky, adults easier to scam."

"My husband used you, planned to take you
hostage,
Six months ago, a Russian girl's courage
Slipped a phone, messaging for aid,
In our despise, a flicker of escape displayed."

I recalled the Instagram message, a lifeline cast,
All the pieces fell, madness amassed.
"Inflamed from the start, this pustule of sin,
A twisted plot, where do I begin?"

"We embalm the bodies after sacrifice," she
screamed,
"To please him, our deity, where nightmares
teemed."
She bowed to the Satanic figure, praying for
grace,
In this twisted den, a sacred place.

But the Russian lady fought with all her might,
Alerted the police, ending the night.
They closed in, but we slipped away,
Shapeshifter hippies, escaping the fray.

Our laughter transcends, a ghostly sound,
Shifting in the night, not to be found.
Now, in a new place, without a trace,
The art studio, our secret base.

The police, they search, but where do they
hound?
In the shadows, lost, not to be found.
Cab de ram, our journey continues on,
In this twisted tale, where darkness dawns.

The Sinister Dance Of Deceit

She opened the window, I saw the light,
Coconut trees swayed, the beach in sight.
Then I questioned, "Why me? I was drowning,
you saved my life!"
"Well, Ananya," she sneered, "you wet whore,
don't cry.
I drugged your beer, pushed you into the sea,
Semi-drowned you, knew you'd develop feelings
for me.
I followed you, earned your trust, every deceitful
move,
Now look where we are, bursting with our
twisted groove.

"Our father will save us, but more blood we
need,
Younger the better, for immortality's greed.
A bloodbath awaits, for our awakened eternity."
His sinister smile, a glimpse of insanity.

Naked they stood, staring stark at me,
He untied the rope, my agony set free.

Grasping my hair tight, pain ignited my brain,
Screams filled the air as I writhed in disdain.

Where would he take me? Shanaya, stout and
strong,
Joined the sinister dance, the unjust prolong.
Kissing me on my lips, tasting my fate,
"Before your sacrifice, a taste we sate."

"From your Instagram, we traced your path,
Announcing your whereabouts a day before,
sealing your wrath.
Tracking you from home to hills, we found ease,
Your love-making session, the perfect tease.

"The rain aided, catching you without a lease,
Tossing your belongings, as you please.
Packed in a garbage bag, your fate sealed tight,
Into our van, to the darkness of the night."

"We sought your virgin soul, of purity, no deceit,
You haven't tricked even a trickster, a feat.
Your heart, pure gold, our sacrificial lamb,
Forgive us, for murdering your soul, for our
damned salvation's calm."

Witnessing Unfathomable Realities

He grasped my hair, my hands untied, dragging
me through the dark,
Where love dared not tread, its essence a spark.
Shanaya, with eyes aflame, followed with lust,
As perverse pleasure in the evil and unknown,
they trust.

My body, once whole, now flawed and scraped,
A naked swan, its purity raped.
White feathers, once pristine, now wilted, torn,
As into the depths of despair, I'm borne.

Into another chamber, I staggered, frail,
Feeling incomplete, lost in a ghastly veil.
Formalin's stench, a sickening mire,
Ropes held bodies, dangling in eerie attire.

Like bats, they hung, women of diverse kind,
If only they were vampires, of a different mind.
Catastrophe and damnation, a dreadful scene,
In the center, a bed, cold and obscene.

A metallic throne, its height adjustable,
On it lay a woman, once so beautiful.
Tall, blonde, and pale, drained of her life's river,
Her blood, a dark tribute to the sinister giver.

The Russian And The Ritual

He seized me by my hair again, a cruel grip,
Lifting me, exposing me to horror's trip.
Pressed my stifled face against the centre bed,
Revealing a woman, her features dread.

Russian, she appeared, a silent plea,
Once cried for help on Instagram's sea.
Regret pierced me, an assumption dire,
Had I acted sooner, spared her from the spiralled
wire.

Naked, the body lay, stripped and bare,
Sutures tracing tales of despair.
"Viscera taken, blood drained," he proclaimed,
Now embalmed, in death's embrace she's
framed.

Shanaya, in reverence, approached with stealth,
Kissing the lips of the embalmed with a
haunting melt.
Whispering chants, a ritual obscure,
Eyes then turned to me, chilling, impure.

The Orbital Love

"Ananya, for a noble cause you stand!
Your name incised in memory, grand!"
With syringe in hand, she approached, near,
Rahul's grip tightened, instilling fear.

In a surge, I felt a sudden might,
A shard of glass gleaming in the dim light.
Hands now freed, a fortuitous mistake,
Adrenaline surged, my will awake.

With a swift motion, glass met air,
Piercing deep, Rahul's eyes to tear.
His chiselled jaw, contorted in pain,
Blood spilled forth, an ominous stain.

Orbital contents, like marmalade, spread,
As he released me, attending to his dread.
Shanaya's wrath, a tempest near,
"You wretch! What have you done?" Shanaya
sneered.

The Grand Detour

I dashed towards the door, desperate for escape,
Into the art studio, a fleeting landscape.
But the door, alas, was locked, sealed tight,
A barrier to freedom, shrouded in far-sight.

I fumbled with the lock, frantic, in vain,
As Shanaya and Rahul closed in, their gain.
Despite his agony, Rahul advanced with speed,
While Shanaya wielded the syringe, her weapon,
her creed.

Into my buttocks, the needle plunged deep,
Its vibrations a sinister secret to keep.
But fate intervened, the needle snapped, _
Embedded in my gluteus, pain overlapped.

With a scream, I retaliated, shard in hand,
Piercing Shanaya's breast, a wound so grand.
Blood gushed forth, a crimson tide,
As she tended her wound, her fury belied.

Unlocking the door, I fled without pause,
Running towards freedom, to escape their claws.

Down the steps to the beach, I hastened my
pace,
To "Pebbles and Caves," a sanctuary's embrace.

Down rocky stairs, into the caves I dove,
A refuge from terror, a haven to rove.
Hoping, praying, for rescue's light,
In the depths of darkness, awaiting flight.

Is Reality Surreal

By the water's edge, my refuge found,
Hoping for rescue, with each patrol's sound.
Their screams intensified, a chilling refrain,
Threats of torture, laced with disdain.

"Ananya, you witch! Where do you hide?
Your flesh and bones, I'll carve inside.
Your agony, my delight to see,
In eternal pain, your soul shall be."

Within a cave, surrounded by rock,
I sought shelter from their relentless mock.
But suddenly, a heaviness did descend,
As if my soul were beginning to transcend.

Had I left my body, in spirit's flight?
Recalling the syringe, its venomous bite.
What drug had they used, to cloud my mind?
From reality's grasp, cruelly unkind.

Was I Dead Or Alive

75

"Shush, little angel, all will be fine,
Your goodness shines, a radiant sign.
Deserving of the best, our pride you are,"
My mother's soothing words, a guiding star.

Then lightning struck, a cruel twist of fate,
My mother gone, leaving sorrow to abate.
A trembling sensation, head heavy with dread,
"Ananya, wake up, it's me," he said.

Through foggy eyes, his form I see,
In a hospital bed, reality dawning on me.
"Where am I?" I murmur, longing for peace,
Aching to rest, fears to release.

In a haze, I realize I'm safe at last,
Saved from the dangers of the past.

Mr. Anorexic?

Mr. Anorexic, defying the fall's might,
Survived the plunge, emerging into light.
A miraculous escape, he claimed to find,
Perhaps the temple's blessing, a force more than
life.

The pandit, witness to our desperate plight,
Summoned aid as day turned into night.
Perched on a rock, near the valley's brink,
The slightest move could have made him sink.

With ropes and courage, rescue drew near,
While a hiker, with valour, cast aside fear.
His grip, tighter than an infant suckling a nipple,
Saved me from the valley's cold, dark space.

Thankful to fate for this chance to thrive,
Saved from the abyss, I feel alive.
Informing the police, our tale we unfold,
Using Google Location, its service bold.

Yes, I confess, I hacked your phone with care,
Using Google Location to track you there.
Your email, your password, known to me,
Your name and zodiac sign, love's decree.

Thinking About The Future

I know I have trespassed, a truth to confess,
But forgive me, my love, now's not the time to
address.
I sought refuge in love, to right my wrongs,
Yet, incompetence revealed, where I truly
belong.

Those fools failed to hide your phone so well,
Its signal traced, a tale to tell.
Into Goa it journeyed, a silent guide,
A glimmer of hope, despite the tide.

Surviving unnoticed till its final stand,
Then disposed of, by careless hand.
But its journey told a story profound,
A machine lost, yet you were found.

The police suspect a cult, with intentions vile,
Gathering the embalmed bodies, matching faces
with missing files.
A hassle indeed, but their racket now crushed,
And you, my love, were the last they hoped to
hush.

So, rejoice, my darling, let's revel in light,
For I'm by your side, holding you tight.
A ring, a symbol of forevermore,
For you, my beloved, I utterly adore.

Shocked and elated, emotions run deep,
Finally, the man who my heart will keep.
In the depths of time, through trials we'll wade,
With you, my love, no fear to evade.

"Marry me," I proclaim, with ardour untamed,
In the hospital ward, our love proclaimed.
Clapping and cheering, witnesses to our bliss,
Never have I felt such utter happiness.

With a kiss, passion ignited, flames soar high,
In that moment, our souls doth fly.
But a nurse's intrusion, a call to refrain,
From public displays, our affection to restrain.

Epilogue

In the hospital's shadow, a peeping tom lurks,
Watching Mr. Anorexic and Ananya, his grin
smirks.
A demonic tattoo adorns his sinister chest,
Heeding the call of his master's behest.

With a call made, to his darkened lord,
"Mom and dad are caught," his voice
underscored.
From an elite, sinister cult they hail,
Controlling the system, their power prevails.

No mercy shown, sacrifices made,
Mom and dad, victims of their charade.
Accepting their fate, without a cry,
On the path to the courthouse, a van would die.

Bombed into oblivion, no chance to survive,
Their final destination, where souls connive.
The grim reapers walk among us, it's true,
Their presence chilling, their intentions askew.

"Trace them to Bangalore, obliterate their mark,
Annihilate them, leave not a single trace.

Decimate all accounts of their earthly existence,
You, the chosen one, possess the talent, the
resistance."

"Yes, master," the ripe one replies with dread,
For the path ahead fills him with death's tread.
To Decimate the new couple before they marry,
Leaving no hope, no chance to tarry.